Dear WORRIED VIOLET...

An Anthology of Advice
Moral, Medical and Miscellaneous

Rosemary Hawthorne

PAVILION

Rosemary Hawthorne is a fashion and social historian and the author of
Knickers: an Intimate Appraisal, *Bras: a Private View*, *Stockings and
Suspenders: a Quick Flash*, *The Costume Collector's Companion 1890–1990*,
and *Do's and Don'ts: an Anthology of Forgotten Manners*.
She is married to a clergyman, they have seven children
and live in Gloucestershire.

First published in Great Britain in 1998 by
PAVILION BOOKS LIMITED
London House, Great Eastern Wharf
Parkgate Road, London SW11 4NQ

Text © Rosemary Hawthorne 1998
Quotations selected by Rosemary Hawthorne

The moral right of the author has been asserted.

Text design and computer page make up by Penny Mills

A CIP catalogue record for this book is available
from the British Library.

ISBN 1 86205 241 7

Printed in Finland by W.S.O.Y.

2 4 6 8 10 9 7 5 3 1

This book can be ordered direct from the publisher. Please contact
the Marketing Department. But try your bookshop first.

Picture Acknowledgments
Cover © Mary Evans Picture Library
All other illustrations courtesy of
Rosemary Hawthorne's private collection.

Contents

Dedicated to the memory of Dorothy Blanche Snow
and all wise and practical Aunts

The author would like to thank magazine editors, then
and now.
Also Judith Mansfield and Ann Morgan-Hughes,
booksellers, for sending treasures from their stock.

Introduction

Have you ever written to a magazine or newspaper seeking some help or advice? You are not alone. For over three hundred years men and women (especially women) have unburdened themselves not only to close relatives, friends, priests, doctors, solicitors and, lately, counsellors, but through the more public avenue of the printed page. People have constantly sought friendly advice for problems great and small from the back-page 'aunties' ~ and 'uncles' ~ who have been in the problem-solving business since the reign of William and Mary, their sensible words flowing freely through three centuries of anxious concern.

The first problem page appeared in a late-seventeenth-century magazine called *The Athenian Gazette* which, after the first edition, became *The Athenian Mercury*. This ran for nearly six years from 1691 and the problem letters it contained were wide-ranging and intellectually stimulating. Significantly, since only a small proportion of people could actually read and write in the seventeenth century, the educated laity did not consider love and sex warranted much debate. Instead, topics such as the mysteries of the Creation, the likelihood of perpetual motion, what caused a rainbow and why a one-hour sermon always seemed longer than two hours' conversation successfully filled the page with an ease that must have brought joy to the editor's heart.

The Athenian's 'advisers' were at first three men: John Dunton, the founder and originator, a printer and bookseller; Richard Sault, a mathematician; and Samuel Wesley (father of the founders of Methodism). Dunton was a shrewd salesman and he marketed the three of them as 'The Athenian Society', which sounded responsible and impressive. Later, other noted writers, including Jonathan Swift and Daniel Defoe, penned lines for this publication and it was not long before the first real 'auntie' was involved on the problem page. Mary Astell was a high-minded bluestocking who wished to found a women's college to 'stock the kingdom with pious and prudent ladies'. Then came 'the refined Lady Masham', known for her virtuous life, elegant phrases and noble thoughts and, finally, Mrs Rowe, a lady poet who wrote stirring, inexplicable stuff such as:

> A friendship so exalted and immense
> A female breast did ne'er before commence.

However, *The Athenian's* combination of talents

proved popular - leaving delighted readers prepared
to purchase 'highlights' from *The Athenian
Mercury*, reprinted as another 'latest' magazine,
The Athenian Oracle.

The early eighteenth century, during the reign of Queen Anne, saw the birth of two classic magazines for the gentry, *The Tatler* and *The Spectator*. Here, editorial spleen was vented on high society, politics and plays, with both journals including elegant satire and amusing, tongue-in-cheek questions and answers, many of them blatantly faked. The editors of both publications, Richard Steele and Joseph Addison, realized the potent value of 'real-life' dilemmas set out in print, reflecting as they did the minor irritations, temptations and exasperations of their upper-class readers.

Later in the eighteenth century, another magazine, *The Female Spectator*, staffed entirely by women, aped the tone set by its male counterpart. It was edited at one point by Mrs Eliza Haywood, a failed actress-cum-journalist and author of romantic novels of a moral nature. So full was her postbag that Mrs Haywood 'recruited' on to her staff three imaginary 'aunties' to deal with the problem page. These were 'Mira', said to be 'clever and harmoniously married'; 'a widow of quality ... who had not buried her vivacity in the tomb ...'; and, lastly, young 'Euphrosine', daughter of a wealthy merchant.

Although by this date an agony aunt might have been *expected* to be female, it was not the case.

Commonly male editors took on the role to write the column that provided its female readers with such sound and delightful advice.

Customers for the magazines still came mainly from the well-to-do, educated classes. After the passing of the Education Act in 1833, however, there was a gradual growth in literacy among the working classes. This led to the publishing of an avalanche of women's magazines, papers and periodicals that continued up to the late 1920s. In these decades we discover the richest vein of anguish, puzzlement, loneliness and bedevilment to which those wise and practical aunts (and uncles) addressed themselves.

It is this amazing, democratic storehouse of assistance that I have plundered to set before you the recorded pains, passions, perplexities and pleasures that expose our inquisitive, uncertain and very human nature.

One or two names or words may appear to be mis-spelt. This is because the publishers, where possible, have remained faithful to the original spelling.

Rosemary Hawthorne
Tetbury, 1998

Moral

This word covers a multitude of sins. It is to do with character or disposition, the distinction between right and wrong, good and evil, the courage to counter odium and contempt as well as being relative to the rules of virtuous behaviour. It can also mean the teaching of a fable, maxim or principle, and be a guide, sense or judgement in human habits, especially sexual.

It is the breastplate of an agony aunt.

Questions and Answers Concerning
Romance, Courtship,
Love, Marriage and
Social Behaviour, including
Matters Touching on Religious Belief

Querist: I had the fortune to be joined in
matrimony to a Man who had another Wife, and
Children by her; which I discovering, brought an
Indictment against him and cast him into the Old
Baillie for his life; after which I begg'd that he
might be transported, which was granted.   Some

time after I had an account of his death and was married some months after his supposed Death to another, and I lived comfortably with him for above two Years, when I received a Letter from my first Husband Courting me for my company, that I may go overseas and live with him. Query, which of the two (if both alive) is my real Husband? Which ought I to follow or ought I to shun both?

Answer: The first was not your Husband before God, he being another Woman's at the time; for God can't be the Author of Adultery nor cou'd he be so in the Eye of the Law; ... so that the Querist can't be at a loss, but must suppose it both Ingratitude and Injustice to leave her last Husband.

The Athenian Oracle, 1697

I know a Gentlewoman who wept the first night she slept with her Husband, whether was it Joy, fear or modesty that caus'd the Tears?

I shall rather attribute it to a fearful Modesty than Joy, or any other Cause, because we find no Instances of Widows who upon their marrying again have wept in going to bed.

The Post Angel, September 1701

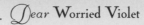

What is more unhappy than an ugly old maid?

It is possible for a handsome young maid to be more unhappy than an ugly old one.

The British Apollo, 1708

Sir, supposing you to be a person of general knowledge, I make my application to you on a particular occasion. I have a great mind to be rid of my wife, and hope, when you consider my case, you will be of opinion I have just pretentions to a divorce. I am a mere man of the town, and have very little improvement but what I have got from plays. I remember in *The Silent Woman*, the learned Dr Cutberd, or Dr Otter, I forget which, makes one of the causes of separation to be 'error personae', when a man marries a women, and finds her not to be the same woman whom he intended to marry, but another. If that be law, it is, I presume, exactly my case. For you are to know, Mr Spectator, that there are women who do not let their husbands see their faces till they are married. Not to keep you in suspense, I mean plainly that part of the sex who paints. They are some of them so exquisitely skilful this way, that give them but a tolerable pair of eyes to set them up with, and they will make bosom, lips, cheeks, and eyebrows by their own industry. As for my dear, never was man so enamoured as I was of her fair forehead, neck and arms, as well as the bright jet of her hair, but, to my great astonishment, I find they were all the effect of art: her skin is so tarnished with this practice, that when she first wakes up in the morning, she scarce seems young enough to be the mother of her whom I carried to bed the night before. I shall take the liberty to part with her by the first opportunity, unless her father will make her portion suitable to her real, not her assumed, countenance. This I thought fit to let him and her know by your means.

I am, Sir, your
most obedient humble servant ...

Mr Spectator replies:
I cannot tell what the law, or the parent of the lady will do for this injured gentleman, but must allow he has very much justice on his side.

Will Honeycomb [a *Spectator* 'character'] told us, one day, an adventure he once had with a lady. She had wit as well as beauty, and made it her business to gain hearts, for no other reason than to rally the torments of her lovers. Her ill-nature and vanity made my friend very easily proof against the charms of her wit and conversation; but her beauteous form instead of being blemished by her falsehood and inconsistency, every day increased upon him, and she had new attraction every time he saw her. When she observed Will irrevocably her slave, she began to use him such, and after many steps towards such a cruelty, she at last utterly banished him. The unhappy lover strove in vain, by servile epistles to revoke his doom; till at last he was forced to the last refuge, a round sum of money to her maid. This corrupt attendant placed him early in the morning behind the hangings in her mistress's dressing-room. He stood conveniently to observe, without being seen. The lady begins the face she designed to wear that day, and I have heard him protest since that she worked a full half-hour before he knew her to be the same woman. As soon as he saw the dawn of that complexion for which he had long languished, he thought fit to break from his concealment ... This lady stood before him in the utmost confusion, with the prettiest smirk imaginable on the finished side of her face, pale as ashes on the other. Honeycomb seized all her gallipots and washes, and carried off his handkerchief full of brushes, scraps of Spanish wool, and phials and unguents.

The lady went into the country; the lover was cured.

The Spectator, January 1710

Mistress: I have the misfortune to be married to a man who spends his life in a regular course of irregularity, and makes no conscience of disturbing me every night at unreasonable hours; he is always the last man in the club room, and when he come home, he reels into the room, talks loud a quarter of an hour and then resigns himself to the sweetest repose which he has so effectively banished from his wife. I seldom see him from noon until after midnight, but am left to pass my evenings, unless relieved by an accidental visit, in the entertaining conversation of a maiden aunt who lives with us. I have proposed separate beds, but he will never hear of it ... I beg you to know whether I may not consider myself as unmarried, and endeavour to lighten the conjugal load, as I see most of my neighbours do; and as I am deprived of my husband's company, admit that of somebody else, for positively I can bear this treatment no longer?

P.S. There is a very pretty gentleman ... who wants to come and chat a few evenings with me. What would you advise?

Before I advise this Lady, I must beg leave to say a word to her husband, and to desire him to consider that if a sentinel will leave his post, he cannot wonder at finding it occupied by another. I sincerely pity her, and if she could punish her husband without hurting herself, should not blame

her.   In the meantime I think the maiden aunt
being with her a happy circumstance and I am
glad to find we are sometimes of use. I can only
recommend her a certain quality which I have
observed to be of real service in the conjugal life, I
mean, patience, for she will certainly find the
remedy she proposed much worse than the disease.

*Mary Singleton, Spinster, Editor of The Old
Maid,* February 1756

Miss Singleton's maidenly advice may possibly
have been greeted with some scepticism when it was
learned that she had forsworn her dedicated spinster
status ... and wed!

Sir: I have for a long time, and still do, retain a
most pure and ardent affection for the most beautiful
of her sex, always endeavouring by every little
service to ingratiate myself in her esteem, or at least
be taken notice of by her. I succeeded in the latter
part of my wishes, in such a manner as made her
sensible I had more than common regard for her.
This discovery only served to make my position
worse as it caused her to avoid my company. Very
lately I was, a few moments, in her company alone.
I made use of the time, as well as the shortness of it
would permit, but met with a repulse; since which
she has avoided me more than ever. I beg your

opinion ... and what course you would advise me to take under my present circumstances?

Sir: Mercutio's advice to Romeo: 'Forget to think of her, take thou some new infection in your heart, and the rank poison of the old will die ...'

Mrs Wentworth, The Court Miscellany,
August 1765

'Mrs Wentworth' was, in reality, Hugh Kelly. A stay-maker by training, then an unsuccessful playwright, he latterly took on editorship of this magazine.

This, Madam, is my own misfortune, to be miserably haunted by a man, whose sight is odious to me: one whom no words can conceive! No denials can satisfy! No affronts affect! Insensible of my uneasiness, and indefensibly increasing it! – I would fly him; but I cannot, unless I would fly my friends too, and my parents, nor have I any intimates left ...

Alas, the gentleman who is so unhappy to be the subject of complaint will be the last to see the force of it. 'Twould certainly be a great happiness if we who love without hope could desist without misery ...

Mrs Grey, The Ladies' Magazine, 1775

Madam, I seek reliable guidance; what should be the conduct of a maiden towards a pleasing gentleman who is not intimate with her family? Could it be taken as an ill-placed gesture to give or receive a good-natured kiss? Please enlighten me.

Distressed One

Child, A touch, a pressure of the hands, are the only external signs a woman can give of entertaining a particular regard for certain individuals. And to lavish this valuable power of expression upon all comers, upon the impudent and contemptible, is an indelicate extravagance which, I hope, needs only to be exposed, to be put ever out of countenance.

As to the salute, the pressure of the lips: that is an interchange of affectionate greeting or tender farewell, sacred to the dearest connections alone. Our parents; our brothers; our near kindred; our bosom's inmate, the friend of our heart's desire; to them are exclusively consecrated the lips of delicacy, and woe be to her who yields them to the stain of profanation.

By the last word, I do not mean the embrace of vice; but merely that indiscriminate facility which some young women have in permitting what they call a *good-natured kiss*. These *good-natured kisses* have often very bad effects, and can never be permitted without injuring the fine gloss of that exquisite modesty which is the fairest garb of virgin beauty.

Be warned! Do not invite invasion of the sanctuary of your lips.

A Lady of Distinction, The Mirror of Graces,
1811

By the 1840s, with easier distribution of goods via the railways, the sales of magazines had increased dramatically, improving yet again in 1848 when W.H. Smith took over the running of station bookstalls with the slogan: 'You can read as you ride.'

From this time, with more letters coming in and less editorial space, it became usual to publish only the aunts' replies. We can perhaps guess at the original lines that brought this stern reprimand:

Sweet Honeysuckle: You act very unadvisedly. No gentleman would wish to associate himself with a woman who runs up debts in so frivolous and selfish a manner. You must control your pursuit of pleasure and extravagant finery and value simpler entertainment and practise thrift. Only then will you be fully trusted as a suitable wife, responsible housekeeper and future mother. If you love this man, avow not to further endanger the betrothal with more needless bills from your milliner.

A Matron, Ladies' Polite Remembrancer, 1843

At this time married women had no rights in law. Once a woman had 'set forth on the ocean of wedlock' all the property, money and independence that had been hers as a spinster passed to her husband. No matter what deprivation, injury or ill-treatment she suffered she was unable to seek any redress in the law. As the law stood, once wed, she became her husband's property. However cruel or unfaithful her spouse, the ignominy of divorce meant that few cases were ever brought – and those desperate women who did were consequently banished, losing not only their titles, homes, possessions and inheritances but also their children.

A DELICATE SUBJECT: We propose the gentleman who signs himself 'Caleb' in the following note as a LOTTERY PRIZE in these stake-loving days; but, before completing our scheme, beg to ask from our fair subscribers their advice with reference to the best means of carrying it out.

Mr. Editor, I shall feel obliged to you for advice *on a delicate subject.* I am a young man with the means of affording a wife every comfort and many luxuries, and have met with many of the fair sex whom I would be too glad to make mine own; but this has been only at places of public resort, such as operas, picture-galleries, horticultural shows, shops, &c.; and I have no means of becoming acquainted with them by formal introductions. I am coxcomb enough to flatter myself that some of these fair creatures are predisposed to receive and return my attentions; and they, too, what are commonly called good matches. What course do you recommend me to pursue? I am, sir, your obedient servant, CALEB.

P.S. I am a gentleman, and my profession one of the highest.

The Lady's Newspaper, October 1848

Sybil: A lady who is introduced to a gentleman at an evening party is not bound to recognize him the next day, even though she had danced with him and conversed on a familiar footing the previous evening. This is one of those laws of politeness wisely framed to protect ladies from those overpowering coxcombs who infest our drawing-rooms.

Cassell's Family Magazine, January 1857

A DELICATE SUBJECT ~ To the Editor: Sir, Your correspondent 'Caleb''s case is puzzling. If he had made choice of one out of his *many*

inamoratas, we might devise some scheme to aid his views; but our ideas of the all powerful 'love' ~ a feeling so subtle in overcoming all obstacles ~ lead us to think somewhat meanly of his abilities. We cannot say that we admire him more for his conceit in imagining these damsels are equally delighted with himself. Let him be sure of possessing the requisite qualities for a good husband, not place his reliance upon his wealth or personal attractions, for they are as dross when compared to the inestimable treasures of the *mind* and *heart*.. Let him, we say, think of all this. Decide upon the one, and then we advise him to adopt the more honourable course of applying *at once* to the mamma of the fair object. With many apologies for our plain-spoken opinions, we remain, sir, your most obedient servants. VERITAS ET FIDES*
**Truth and Faith*

> *The Lady's Newspaper,* November 1848

A Wife's Duties. ~ A wife should endeavour to make her home as comfortable as possible, so that her husband may always look forward with pleasure to the time when he reaches home. That system of gossiping ... when a woman exposes her husband's failings, she breaks her marriage vow ... Whatever may be the private character of her

husband, it should be defended rather than laid open to attack.

The Family Friend, 1852

This next reply was printed one month before the Divorce Bill came into effect in January 1858.

E.J.T. ~ However disgraceful the bridegroom's conduct may have been in deserting his bride, it does not exonerate her from her duties and his claim. She cannot marry again; nor, unless she is a bolder woman than ordinary, would she, after past experience, wish it.

Cassell's Family Magazine, December 1857

Lizzie: Your friends are much to blame in encouraging you in hopes that can only end in disappointment. We do not doubt you are very pretty and that you make a good match, but you are likely to die a spinster if, in spite of your being an uneducated member of the working classes, you can be satisfied with nothing less than a clergyman.

Cassell's Family Magazine, October 1860

Julia: Love, as we know it, is bold; but vice bolder, and always prefers secrecy – it cannot exist in the sunshine of honour and candid explanation.

Florence: You write about a fourteen years' courtship, and complain that for a long time the dawdling swain has not replied to your letters. The sensible course for you would be to consider him dead, or married, or if neither, not worth your having.

The London Journal, 1862

Governesses frequently popped out to post letters to agony aunts, since their status as dependent, middle-class spinsters often made them sad victims of social and financial problems.

> Poor Governess (Brighton): We pity you; such people are not Christians; they are infidels, who profane the name of religion. Even the Russians – who we regard as benighted – set us an example in their way of treating governesses.
>
> *Cassell's Family Magazine*, 1862

> Louisa A., Who tells us she can play the piano, draw, and make herself useful, has been in love several times, but in every instance her attachment has been unrequited. She wants a husband, and applies for a recipe to get one; also for removing pimples on the face.

> The best way to get a husband is not to look for one. The second question is more grave. Pimples on the face generally indicate a bad state of body – just as harping on the subject of beaux shows a bad state of mind. The best plan is to take advice from a medical man about the pimples, and from some lady friend of good common sense about the sweethearts.
>
> *'Conversazione', The Englishwoman's Domestic Magazine*, 1867

This monthly magazine was at first owned and
edited by Samuel Beeton, husband of Isabella, the
author of the famous book on Household Manage-
ment.

Minnie: No decent woman ever tampers with
'matrimonial advertisements'. There is no
occasion for such to advertise for a husband. It is
the refuse of the market which is put up for
auction ...

The Home Magazine, c. 1870

Amorous Fanny: Are these following lines the
ones you mean? We do not know the name of
the author.

The Wish of a Bachelor

1 Gentle companion to soften my cares,
2 Thousand a year to conduct my affairs,
3 Dogs and a gun to pass away time,
4 Horses and chaise to convey me and mine,
5 Cheerful companions ~ wise, prudent, and
    merry,
6 Dishes each day, with six glasses of sherry,
7 Beds to accommodate friends at their leisure,
8 Somethings or other to add to their pleasure,

9 Pounds in my pocket when cash I require,
And a passport to heaven when from earth I
retire.

The Young Ladies' Journal, 1872

Notice to Correspondents

We cannot undertake to reply to correspondents by letter. All ladies wishing their questions answered must use signatures of an unobjectionable kind. We decline to answer any who adopt either vulgar or slang signatures.

Harry's Little Puss: A young lady should not correspond with a gentleman, nor send a photograph of herself, not even at his request, unless she is engaged to him.

An Ignorant One: The third finger of the left hand.

A Distressed Aunt: Marriage by Register is as legal as any other form of marriage.

Stupid **L**ittle **M**iss **C**uriosity: **I**t is not at all the custom, and *never* has been, for a lady to kiss a gentleman under the mistletoe. **T**he following is the origin: it was customary in olden times for the rich and noble to treat their dependants at **C**hristmas and to meet them on terms of equality, considering that all men are regarded alike by the religion of **H**im whose natal day they are celebrating. **A** sort of licence prevailed. **T**herefore, a branch of mistletoe was hung in the hall or doorway, and the youths – of all classes – were understood to have a right to kiss any maiden whom they could inveigle under it.

Saucy **E**liza and **W**ild **R**ose: **I**f you will send a stamped, addressed envelope, we will accede to your request. **W**e *certainly never* answer questions of this kind in our **C**orrespondence pages.

All from *The Young Ladies' Journal,* 1875

Forget-**M**e-**N**ot: **H**ad you asked advice before your engagement, we should have endeavoured to dissuade you from marrying one to whom religion appears distasteful. **B**ut now your marriage is about to take place ... you should let him know, now at once, how far above all earthly affection is the love of Jesus, the Redeemer, and that it will be a sore trial for you, if you do not have him (*your husband*) accompany you to church on Sunday.

Darkness: We think that a past engagement of nine years, and a future one lasting two or three years more, is calculated to try the affections of any man or woman. Under the circumstances, you had better give him his freedom, however hard it may be for you; but if he is an upright man, he should prefer to keep his promise to you, seeing you have given him your youth in patient waiting.

Perplexed Girl: If you intend to become his wife, we see no objection, as he has every right to ask you to improve yourself, both before and after marriage.

J.'s Pussy: We are glad to hear you are only seventeen, as you appear to have very little idea of propriety. At your age you cannot decide for yourself ... either write, or say very distinctly what we have said, and that you are deeply distressed that you have already been so deceitful and disobedient to the parents who trust you.

Country Bumpkin: A flirt is one who keeps up a bantering, jesting intercourse with men ~ a sort of undignified and spurious lovemaking, tending to mislead as to her serious intentions. Your handwriting is not yet formed.

Nervous Gertrude: Does your mother know of your engagement to the young man with whom you take walks? At the same time, do not deceive your mistress, and should she enquire whether you were walking with a fellow servant, take care to speak the truth.

Karl: Your letter was of the class that should have gone into the waste-paper basket. Semiramis (not 'mus') was a queen of Assyria. She was assassinated, by her son, in 1990 BC for gross immorality.

Scholastica: Does not seem to take natural attraction into account. 'Love is given, not bought.' She might be very strongly attracted and love another girl very warmly, but that other girl might feel no such attraction or love for her; nor do we think she could find fault with her for anything so natural, over which she had no control.

All from *The Girls' Own Paper,* 1881 and 1885

Launched in 1880 by the Religious Tract Society, *The Girls' Own Paper* was at this time edited by a clergyman, the Reverend T.B. Willson, MA.

'There is much in our paper, we humbly believe, that will train our girls in living a pure and honest life ... From our daily letters ... some written upon coroneted notepaper by those of noble birth and by others from the kitchens ... our paper has given them a high aim in their lives and a practical and wise assistance ...'

Broken-hearted: We cannot really undertake to advise you as to what is your best course. Yours is a peculiar case. It is rare for any one person to be simultaneously threatened with epilepsy, deserted by her affianced lover after the banns have been published, bitten by a dog, which had been rendered insane through being led about by a string, expelled from her lodging for non-payment of rent and thrown out by an active volcano. These events do not often happen together. Do not, at any rate, return the presents your lover gave you. If we were in your place, we should convert them into cash. Then you might take out a County Court Summons against the owner of the dog, also the volcano, and have something over for a Breach of Promise action.

Punch, 1887

No governess should advertise her willingness to do light housework ... I would advise you to leave your present position; you could scarcely be in a worse one, and you might do better. There are reasonable employers who recognize their duty to their subordinates.

The Young Woman, 1895

This next selection of letters comes from a popular magazine of the 1890s, *Home Sweet Home*, answered by 'Aunt Marjorie' who offered 'Advice to Our Readers on their little Personal Affairs'.

'Daisy' says: I am eighteen and know a man whom I have met very often, when I go away each season to the sea. He lives there, and my family go nearly every season. I have fallen deeply in love with him, and I know he admires me, for he has told me so, and is very polite, but nothing more. Do you think he is showing any signs that some day he may ask me to be his wife? Nobody knows I love him, but when anyone jokes us about each other, we both blush.

I am afraid, dear, the fact of his blushing is not sufficient to tell you, or me, whether he will ever want to marry you. You must just have patience till he gives you far greater proofs of caring.

W. and R. write: Do you think we are incapable of feeling real love at seventeen and eighteen? We believe ourselves to be tenderly and devotedly in love with two charming girls of about the same age, but they laugh at the idea of love at that age in our sex, and call us boys.

They are quite wrong. Youths of your age are capable of being very desperately in love.

Passion Flower asks: What am I to do, dear Aunt Marjorie? I am in love with a soldier, but the other night after a ball, he rushed down the steps and shouted 'Good night, my darling girl!' This he did in the presence of some twenty or thirty people, who were waiting for their carriages. How can a man do such a thing unless he was drunk, and ought I to encourage him any more?

A gentleman should never so far forget himself. And a man who takes too much wine is not calculated to make any woman happy as his wife. You might speak to him about it, and if ever he repeats the offence, I should give him up without any hesitation.

Country Cousin says: I am twenty-five years of age, and hold a good position out here in the country. But Nature is unkind in one particular respect: she is slow to find me a wife, and as I do not move much in society, I am beginning to feel I am doomed to run for life in single harness. Can you recommend me some nice quiet watering-place where there would be a possibility of my meeting a future wife?

I am truly sorry for this lonely bachelor. But why want to go to a quiet place? I should think one where he might see many would be the most likely to suit his requirements. Why not try Scarborough or Brighton?

Slighted says: How could I win the love of a man? I had a lover from August to December last year, then I met him with other girls, and I gave him up. I should much like to have another lover, if you can tell me in what way I can get one?

That is a question no one can answer for you, dear. Be more particular whom you choose next time, that's all.

Distracted Lover: What an extraordinary story! You say you love a girl whose father is an anarchist and he will not let you marry her unless you become an anarchist, too. You ask should you become one, which is against your principles, or elope?

My good friend, never do anything against your principles, no matter what. Neither can I advise you to elope, even under these peculiar circumstances. Try patience.

A.B.C.: The widower who is paying you attention seems to me to be doing so in a very underhand way. I should certainly not take the steps he wishes you to do. If he thinks it too soon after his wife's death to be publicly engaged again, it is certainly too soon for him to carry on like this in secret.

Lonely Tottie: I have a dear friend who is most anxious to hear our minister preach. Would there be anything wrong in offering to take him into our pew? I go to church alone each Sunday; but I am well-known there, and I am afraid that if I took this friend people might talk.

It would certainly look a little marked if you and he went to church and sat alone in the pew together. Could you not get some lady friend to go too?

Home Sweet Home, 1893–1894

Such a splendid man – one I have known for over a year – has asked me to marry him. I said 'yes', and my people consented two days ago, but I have false teeth and wear a false fringe and it seems to me I'm not the girl he thinks me. What shall I do?

If it is sufficient to alter his feelings towards you, they must have little foundation. Tell him certainly ... but as I suppose he cares for you, and not for your teeth and hair, I cannot see how the revelation will greatly affect him.

Forget-Me-Not, 1898

Japonica: We do not see how 'Japonica' can require *advice* on such a subject. Most girls of eighteen have some knowledge of the rules of propriety; and if in doubt as to allowing stray young men to kiss her (ignorance which we do not believe), she can consult any older person – her mother or one of her brothers. We often think that such letters are written by foolish and vain girls to show off. There could be no other motive for writing to us about such a subject.

Girls' Own Paper, 1899

Young Bride-to-Be: Never enter on the secret
duties of a wife unless you can give to him whose
name you take, an honest, wholehearted affection.
I can speak from experience ...

Girls' Own Paper, 1903

This magazine was now edited by a woman, Flora
Klickmann.

Widowed One: Yours is a very sad story. After
six years of widowhood, to meet and love a man
who also loves you but who would not consent to
your crippled son sharing his home if you become
his wife, is very hard indeed on you. Your duty
is, most definitely, with your child.

The Cosy Corner, 1906

Pegasus: My age is thirty-three and I have never
been in love until now. By profession I am an
artist, portraiture is my talent, and I have seen
many beautiful women in the capacity of models.
With them, I have never flirted nor behaved
other than as though I worked before the whole
world. But now I have fallen completely in love
with a sweet young girl of nineteen who sat for my
last picture in my studio in Chelsea. I admired

her from the first day, but now I care for her as I never knew it was in the power of a man to care for a woman. As yet I have not declared my love for her ~ one reason I am a little shy, and for another I have heard that she is living in some dreadful locality, that her father is often inebriated, that her mother often stitches for a firm of tailors and that this girl has been in the chorus of a theatre and only acts as model when out of a theatrical engagement. Yet she is every inch the lady to speak to, and to know her is to love her.

Can you offer a chap, situated as I am, a word of friendly advice?

I am afraid, my dear chap, that like all those who have experienced the fever of love in their mature years, you have it worse than others who may have been assailed by milder attacks beforehand. Of course, it is not necessary for me to inform you that artists' models are not, as a rule, persons of great repute. Remember, beauty is but skin deep. Ask yourself, 'Is my love of such strength that I can cherish my beloved when it is no longer her Springtime?' As to her surroundings, she is not responsible for these, or for the too-free libations in which her paternal parent is wont to indulge. One sometimes finds a thing of beauty amongst the most objectionable surroundings. I can only advise you to be cautious before compromising your word of honour. Having assured yourself that the lady is all that you deem her to be, marry her as speedily as you can and move her away from her family influences. Good luck go with you in your wooing.

Social Confidences by Valentine, Enquire Within, Ladies' Home Journal, 1912

Dear Amor, Would you help me a little? I have been out with a gentleman for about a year; he is far above my position, and my friends all say he does not want me. I must say I love him very much, and he always seems very affectionate. He begins all his letters with 'My dearest', and ends, 'Your own boy'. My parents have dared me to go with him. His age is twenty-two, mine twenty-one. Do tell me what to do, Amor. Hoping to see a reply as soon as possible.

Yours, Broken-Hearted N.B.

Answer: If there is a great difference in social position the affair is likely to lead to unhappiness and you would be wise to listen to your parents.

Tearful Tibbie: The boy is fickle and not worth troubling about, besides being much too young to think about marrying. Occupy your mind with other things, and join a girls' club.

Troubled Edith: Tell him the truth about your age now before you marry. Think of the trouble you may bring on yourself later by your deceit.

Autumn Berry: Seeing the good advice you give, I made up my mind to write and ask your advice concerning my first love affair. Nine months ago I met a young fellow and his chum at my aunt's. They were both in the same regiment and billeted with her. I stayed three weeks. When I returned home they both asked if they might write to me, and also asked me to write to them and send them my photo. My parents gave their consent, so I wrote to them in a sisterly way ~ and they replied. About a month ago I met them again, and they have been to my home and my parents like them very much. One of them is just like a brother to me, but the other one is changed, and has asked me to become engaged to him. When I first met him I did not like him very much, but since I have seen him again I do like him very very much indeed, and I want to make him happy. He told me he loves me and has never had a girl before. I have never been in love, and do not know if I am really and truly in love with him now, or if it is only sisterly love. I always feel very happy after receiving his letters and also when I am with him. Please tell me if I am in love or not. What would you advise me to do? I told him I would give him his answer in three weeks' time, when he is going to have four days' leave. Our ages are – his twenty-two next week, and my own twenty-one in October.

Answer: You ought to know your own feelings better than Amor can tell you, Autumn Berry. You must give up the correspondence with the other. Does this help you?

From *Amor's Courtship Column, Our Home,*
1912, 1913 and 1915

During the 1914–18 War there was less correspondence regarding love and romance in magazines; lifeline letters were sent to the beloveds instead. The huge death toll from the war made editors aware that printed letters of this nature would seem insensitive to those thousands of women who had lost husbands and boyfriends at the Front. But there are many letters similar to this next one.

I have lost my dear, brave soldier boy, and all my friends and also his family are angry with me because I do not wear black. But neither he nor I approve of mourning; he always begged me never to put it on for him, and so I do not. He loved me best in white, and when I can wear it, I

think of him and long for him to be with me
again. But it is so hard to be looked on as
heartless that I have nearly given way more than
once. Do you think I ought to do so?

No, my dear, I do not. You are showing as
much respect to his memory by doing as he
preferred and as you promised, as by wearing the
deepest symbols of woe. Time will accustom
people to your opinions, and you will have the
satisfaction of knowing that you kept your word
and did as he would have wished. My very true
and deep sympathy in your loss. May you
receive comfort to go on with life and its duties as
bravely as did your hero boy.

Forget-Me-Not, 1915

As the war continued the huge loss of life numbed
the social senses and our auntie was soon writing:

Nowadays mourning is greatly shortened and
even, in some cases, not worn at all.

Forget-Me-Not, 1916

After the war, normal agony communications resumed:

Fretful Phyllis: I have been friendly with a boy for about four months. He takes me for walks and rides on his motor bike, but he has never spoken of love. We have known one another by sight all our lives, as our families attend the same church. People are beginning to talk, and ask when will we become engaged. He is twenty and I am twenty-one. Are we too young to speak of love?

Unless a boy of twenty be in a good position, it is not right for him to ask for a girl's love. It is absurd for people to question you about your engagement. Don't pay any heed to such enquiries, but be glad to accept the friendship offered. It is impossible for me to say if it will ripen into love ...

Undecided Maud: I have two boys, one is dark and the other fair. The fair one lives far away, and I do not see him often. I go with the other often and like him best, but the fair one loves me better. Which one do you think I ought to care for most?

I think you will be happier with the dark one, lassie, and I expect the other one will soon forget if you make no arrangements to see him or correspond. Your own heart is better able to answer than I.

Older Friend: I have had an offer of marriage from a man sixty years of age. My own is eighteen. This is a very serious question which I cannot decide without good advice. He is loving, thoughtful and handsome, but I do not know if I could be happy with him.

You would be most unwise to agree to this union. Forty-two years' difference in age is too great to contemplate. Personally, I should always be strongly opposed to a young girl sacrificing her youth in such a way.

Bubbles: I go out regularly once a week with my Cousin Jack. Unfortunately, there are constant quarrels in his house because his brother objects to his going with me. My parents also raise objections. How am I to know if he loves me, and can first cousins marry?

It is legal for cousins to marry, but inadvisable for hereditary reasons.

Shy Girlie From Wales: I am only nineteen, but I don't think I shall ever have a sweetheart. I'm so shy when in the company of the other sex. I hardly say anything and look away when they look at me. As I go everywhere on my own, I should so much like to have a sweetheart. Do you think I should be more forward?

Be less reserved, lassie, but not 'forward'. Don't confuse modesty with bashfulness. No girl should forsake modesty and make herself cheap in order to attract the opposite sex. Interest in others is one of the best means of overcoming shyness. You'll soon be writing to tell me about your sweetheart, I expect, dear.

Sad Sally: I have been married eighteen months. For the first three months we were happy. After that my husband's people interfered; they told him lies about me and are always coming round to the house, and have thoroughly upset everything. I am miserable because I still love him, but I am convinced he has lost all affection for me. I have done my duty to him, but feel I must do as my mother suggests, take my kiddie and leave him. Please advise me?

It grieves me to learn of your unhappiness, dear, but try to go on living with your husband and you may win him back yet. Your husband can claim the child by law if you left him. For the little one's sake try to struggle on, bearing your heartache.

All from *Peggy's Post Bag, Peggy's Own Paper,*
1919–21

Jealous: Is jealousy a fault or a misfortune? I find that someone else has only to look at my beloved and I feel actually sick with jealousy.

In your case it certainly is a fault and you should try to overcome it. A certain amount of jealousy is inevitable, but there should be adequate cause for it to be aroused.

Isabel, Home Notes, 1920

Bashful Benny: I am in a great state of indecision. I have every chance of marrying a wealthy, middle-aged lady who appears to have a very definite affection for me. I am twenty-four, and though I do not love this woman, do you think I should be doing wrong by proposing marriage which will mean my personal advancement?

I think before you propose, you should make sure that she really thinks of matrimony. Many middle-aged women like a young man as a friend, but would resent being thought in love with him. I never like to hear of a young man, or woman, marrying for money. It is very wrong.

Mrs Marryat Advises, Woman's Weekly, 1922

Working Girl Susan: I have been engaged for some time, and we can't really afford to marry just yet. We have heard of some unfurnished rooms, though, which would just suit us, and I feel we ought to take this chance as they are so difficult to get. If I went on working we could manage to marry, and I should like to do this, but everyone I know says that married women oughtn't to work, and that it only spoils the husband and prevents him from getting on. What do you think?

Get married and keep on with your work, but make this a temporary arrangement. Do try to save for a home of your own. It is only when wives keep on working to escape from the responsibility of a home and children that I think it is wrong for them to do so. Make it clear to your husband from the beginning that you want to leave off working as soon as possible, and I am sure he will try hard to get on, and bring the happy day nearer.

Muriel, The Lady's Companion, 1923

Heartbroken: I am sorry to hear of your great
unhappiness, Jeanne, yet I believe in the end that
the average English girl leads a more contented life
if she is married to an *Englishman*. You have
been unable to revive the interest of this foreign
boy, so now you should give the English boy a
chance. People who have had no disappointments
rarely develop interesting personalities, dear, and
you will always have romantic memories to look
back upon, whatever the future holds. It is better
than a colourless life.

Married Another Girl: I am breaking my heart
with longing for him, and I don't even know if
he's happy or not.

I expect he is, dear, now that they have their baby;
and he married her of his own free will. It was a
cruel trick on her part to bet that she could take him
from you, but now she has done so you will only
make her feel more triumphant if you let her see
your misery. And your friends will begin to talk.
Try to go out with any nice boy who asks you.

In Despair (Hants): He has a bad reputation in the village and all my friends warn me against him, but he keeps asking me to let him take me for a ride. He says he's not as bad as he's painted and asks me to trust him.

Then arrange to go with him one afternoon so that you can be home again before dark. And map out some definite programme and ask him to take you to some definite place of interest. If you keep him on the move, he'll have less time for anything else.

All from *Modern,* 1925

Governesses still had problems ...

Old Maid: I would so like to marry, but get no opportunities. I am a nursery governess, and have been unfortunate in the men that I have met.

Get a pen-friend. Couldn't you join a rambling club?

Home Notes, 1926

Medical

'Of the healing art ...'
The Concise Oxford Dictionary

WHEN quackery abounded and doctors'
fees were expensive, or facing up to a real
doctor was worse than the affliction (of
what century do I write, I wonder?) the trust
placed in any printed word under the term 'medical'
was knowledge imbued with an authority to be
sought, savoured, read and re-read by those in sore
need of help or relief in their distress. The role of
the medical auntie was awesome with responsibility.
Nothing changes.

Questions and Answers Concerning
*Physical and Mental
Complaints
(Serious and Trivial), including
Effective Cures and Suggestions*

for Well-Being

Gentlemen, I am a young gentlewoman in the
prime of my youth, and if my glass flatters me
not, tolerably handsome, likewise co-heiress of a
very fair estate; there being two sisters of us to
enjoy what my aged father hath. He hath ever

shown himself lovingly tender, yet he hath ever
had so great an awe over us that we shall never
durst give him the least suspicion of any ill-
conduct of our behaviour, he often assuring us that
nothing should so quench the flame of his paternal
love, as our deviation from the strict rules of pure
charity and its handmaid, modesty. Now to my
utter ruin and eternal shame, I am now with
child; how, when and by whom to my greatest
grief I know not; but this I also know too well,
that the hour wherein my father hears of it, I am
disinherited of his estate, banished of his love ...
Gentlemen, I earnestly implore you to give me
some relief by solving these two queries:

1. Whether it be possible for a Woman to so
carnally to know a man in her sleep as to conceive
for I am sure this, and no other way was I got
with child?

2 Whether it may be lawful to use means to put
a stop to this growing mischief and ... kill it in
the embryo; this being the only way to avert the
thunderclap of my father's indignation?

To the first question, Madam, we are very
positive that you are mistaken, for the thing is
absolutely impossible if you know nothing of it;
indeed, we had an account of a widow that made
such a pretence, and she might have better credit
than a maid, who can have no plea but dead
drunk or in some kind of swooning fit, and our

physician will hardly allow the possibility even then. As for your second query, such practices are murder and those that are so unhappy as to come under such circumstances, if they use the fore-mentioned means will certainly find the remedy worse than the disease. There are wiser methods to be taken in such cases – as a small journey and a confidant. And afterwards such a pious and good life as may redress such a heavy misfortune.

A lady of extraordinary shape ... but inclining to be fat ... fears her fat may grow excessive, and therefore desires your advice, what should she do in that case? Will you prescribe a method for obtaining her desire ... that is, stopping or rather lessening her fat?

It is needless to prescribe many things where fewer will do. Therefore if the lady confines herself to make her breakfasts and suppers for a month or two of water-gruel, made only with a little oatmeal, this diuretic gruel will discharge and sensibly diminish the superfluous fatness.

Both from *The Athenian Oracle, c.* 1697

What is the reason when a Woman cuckolds her
husband, the child is commonly like the father?

Pray ~ whom shou'd a child resemble sooner than
his father?

The British Apollo, c. 1700

To Mr. Bickerstaff: I am much afflicted with
the gravel, which makes me sick and peevish. I
desire to know of you, is it reasonable that any of
my acquaintances should take advantage over me at
this time, and afflict me with long visits, because
they are idle and I am confin'd. Pray, Sir,
reform the town in this matter ...

Mr Bickerstaff replies: It is with some so hard a
thing to employ their time, that it is a great good
fortune when they have a friend indispos'd that
they may be punctual in perplexing him, when he
is recover'd enough to be in that state which
cannot be call'd sickness or health, when he is too
well to deny company and too ill to receive 'em.
It is no uncommon case, if a man is of any figure
or power in the world, to be congratulated into a
relapse.

The Tatler, c. 1710

Some Regency Health Tips:

Madam Recammier's Pommade

This was communicated by this lady as being used in France and Italy, by those who professionally, or by choice, are engaged in exercises which require long and great exertions of the limbs ...

Take any suitable quantity of *Axungia Cervi*, i.e. the fat of the red stag or hart; add to it the same quantity of olive oil (Florence oil is preferable to any of the kind), and half the quantity of virgin wax; melt the whole in an earthen vessel, well-glazed, over a slow fire, and when properly mixed, leave it to cool. This ointment has been applied also with considerable efficacy in cases of need.

Eau des Carmes

This water has been of a very long-standing in repute with nearly everybody on the Continent; it was invented by a Carmelite Friar. It is of great assistance in lowness of spirits, in rheumatic pains, and for gout in the stomach.

Take one quart of brandy, and infuse into it cinnamon, cloves, and angelica root, of each half an ounce; coriander seeds, nutmegs grated, one ounce of each; a quarter of a pound of balm leaves, and two ounces of lemon peel; put the whole into a crucible, and let it stand near the fire three days; then mix with it one pint of balm water, and distil it over a slow fire; drain off the liquor, and let it be well corked up in bottles for the space of one month before you make use of it.

To assuage the raging pain of a Corn by instant application:

Take equal parts of a roasted onion and soft soap, beat them up together, and apply them to the corn in a linen rag by way of poultice.

All taken from 'A Lady of Distinction', *The Mirror of Graces*, 1811

From *Enquire Within*

An Unhappy Woman: A few suggestions to relieve you from your constant state of depression ... The safest and best of all occupations for such sufferers as are fit for it, is intercourse with young children. Next to this comes honest, genuine acquaintanceship with the poor ...

A Dublin Doctor: Unless you can control your passions, the sooner you quit the medical profession the better. Temptation, we know, is very powerful; even the good St Anthony could not resist the witchery of a pair of laughing black eyes ... When in the throes of your distemper, think, upon all occasions attempt to impart vigour to the tone of your mind, and, depend upon it, you will gradually become more cool and collected in your deportment.

Both from *The London Journal,* 1845 and 1849

A Young Mother: The smile on the face of infants sleeping is more likely to be an indication of worms in the bowels than of any communion with the world of spirits. Try a little salt in its food. This simple condiment affords certain relief from such parasitical vermin.

Adela: It does so happen that we were among a chosen few of a medical school, in the neighbourhood of Bilston, selected to proceed to that town during the prevalence of the cholera in 1832, when the resident medical men were found unequal to the heavy duties the extent of the disease imposed. We, therefore, had opportunities in becoming acquainted with every practice recommended; and every specific proclaimed, one after the other, proved decided failures. The only treatment ultimately adopted was the simple mustard emetic, made by mixing a tablespoonful and a half in a tumbler of warm water, and drinking largely of that fluid at the same time to promote sickness. It is not a disagreeable emetic at all. A powder of calomel and opium was afterwards given; but as these are not medicines that should be taken without proper advice, in case they are required, we recommend a medical man to be sent for immediately. We are much interested in our fair correspondent's very long letter.

Pussey Margotte: A little *citron* ointment will do your eyes good. You will make them worse by shaving the hairs on your forehead.

Azella: Do not think about your looks in church, and you will feel less of the inconvenience alluded to. However, avoid all slops in your diet.

A Constant Subscriber: A gargle, made by infusing ten grains of Cayenne pepper in half a pint of water should do good.

Scarletina and True Blue: Attention to the state of the bowels, and a generous diet, would best meet the circumstances.

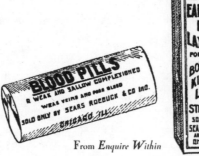
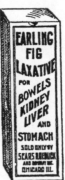

From *Enquire Within*

Lucy Neal: Perhaps tea may not agree with you. We have noticed that new bread in such cases as yours is very apt to occasion the unpleasantness complained of.

A Constant Subscriber: How old? Married or single and do you wear your stays tightly laced? We should say you were past twenty-five, unmarried, and aim at having a fine figure; but cannot advise on mere supposition.

Lady Geraldine Neville: You can obtain the elastic kneecaps from any French corset-maker.

Blanche: The extension exercises, skipping, and dumb-bells would correct the malformation. Leave the spot alone.

Henrietta: The cause of the infirmity is the advanced age of your friend. The use of a magnet to suspend such natural progress of mortality is absurd, and not at all consistent with that resignation which should mark the thoughts of one who can number, of years, threescore and ten.

An Admirer: At least once a week. In all well-regulated nurseries, Saturday night is usually termed 'washing night', and the children, all round, are treated to a home bath and a laxative dose.

Augusta: We advise no exposure at all. Wear long sleeves, with gloves, and a very thick silk handkerchief around the neck.

An Orphan: Try half an ounce of sulphur and the same quantity of carbonate of iron, mixed in half a pound of treacle. A large teaspoonful every other morning for a week. Report progress.

Julia: We cannot say of what composition artificial teeth are made. Those of ivory are best, only they do not preserve their colour.

Anxious Madonna: Try a warm bath at the critical season, and take some gentle aperient medicine. Write again and say what effect.

Mal-A-Tête: Shall be answered next week. In the meantime, apply a little *citron* ointment to allay irritation.

Mary: A case requiring much consideration. See next week's paper.

Next week's replies:

Mal-A-Tête: The evil is a serious one, and we recommend you to consult a properly qualified practitioner without delay.

Mary: Cupping at the back of the neck would do you a great deal of good. Your medical adviser takes a correct view of your case. You will never get well unless you overcome the despondency under which you labour.

Busy Bee: In childhood it is very natural. Every new plaything is seized so as to crush and destroy it. On the slightest check, it is usual for their limbs to stiffen as with a strong spasm. They sometimes grow up little furies, screaming and choking under their own frightful fits of rage. It is difficult to recommend any proper discipline, but a mother's observation will soon discover means of restraint, by depriving them of little indulgences under circumstances of bad temper. It is very unwise, however, to give them *anything to be good* – a very common error in nurseries.

Lady Clemence: Animal food and a glass of stout twice a day. You are improving.

A.S.F.: Yours is the most extraordinary case. Avoid all strong medicines and violent exercise. Keep your mind calm, and have a shower-bath every morning, at the temperature of 75 degrees. Report progress.

All taken from *The Lady's Newspaper,*
1848 and 1849

Sea-Bathing: To have the greatest benefit from sea-bathing, it is proper to remain but a very short time in the water – not exceeding two or three minutes ... On coming out, the body should be wiped dry with a rough cloth and the ordinary dress resumed as quickly as possible.

The Family Friend, 1852

For those Hasty Treatments Needed by Travellers in Foreign Parts

An Emergency Emetic: For want of proper physic, drink a charge of gunpowder in a tumblerful of warm water or soapsuds, and tickle the throat with a feather.

The Art of Travel, Sir Francis Galton, 1867

A Lady from Edinburgh: I have been abroad for the past four years, during which time I left my daughter at a large and fashionable boarding-school near London; I sent for her home directly I arrived, and ... I expected to see a fresh rosy girl of seventeen come bounding to welcome me. What, then, was my surprise to see a tall, pale young lady glide slowly in with measured gait and languidly embrace me? When she had removed her mantle,

I understood at once what had been mainly instrumental in metamorphosing my merry romping girl into a pale, fashionable belle. Her waist had ... been reduced to such absurdly small dimensions that I could easily have clasped it with my two hands. 'How could you be so foolish,' I exclaimed, 'as to sacrifice your health for the sake of a fashionable figure?' 'Please don't blame *me*, Mamma,' she replied, 'I assure you I would not have voluntarily submitted to the torture I have suffered for all the admiration in the world.' She then told me of how the most merciless system of tight-lacing was the rule of the establishment, and how she and her forty or fifty fellow-pupils had been daily imprisoned in the vices of whalebones drawn tight by the muscular arms of sturdy waiting-maids. The mischief is done; her muscles have been murdered, and she must submit for life to be encased in a stiff panoply of whalebone and steel; and all this for what? Merely to attract admiration for her small waist. I write to you and inform your readers of the system adopted in fashionable boarding-schools, so that if they do not wish their daughters tortured into wasp-waist invalids they may avoid sending them to schools where the corset-screw is an institution of the establishment.

The Englishwoman's Domestic Magazine,
March 1867

Subsequently, for several months in the Englishwoman's Domestic Magazine there were other
letters, for and against the practice of tight-lacing.
During a prim period it was an obvious, titillating
thrill for Victorian readers.

Here are some excerpts:

> Staylace: In reply to the lady from Edinburgh
> ... A waist 'easily clasped with two hands'. Ye
> powers, what perfection! how delightful! ... ever
> since I have read that I have worn a pair of stays
> that I had rejected as too small for me, as they did
> not quite meet behind ... and have submitted to an
> extra amount of *muscular exertion* from my maid,
> in order to approach ... the delightful dimensions
> of two handfuls ...

> Nora: I venture to trouble you with a few
> particulars on ... 'tight-lacing' ... your March
> number inviting correspondence on the matter. I
> was placed at the age of fifteen at a fashionable
> school in London, and there it was the custom for
> the waists of the pupils to be reduced one inch per
> month until they were what the lady principal of
> the school considered small enough. When I left
> ... at seventeen, my waist measured only thirteen
> inches, it having been formerly twenty-three inches
> ... it was often a subject of great rivalry among the
> girls to see which could get the smallest waist ...

A Constant Subscriber: I may be able to give a little comfort to the mother of the unfortunate victim of tight-lacing. I knew a precisely similar case ~ a girl whose waist was thirteen inches round at seventeen ~ that was ten years ago ~ it now measures twenty-two inches, and I believe her recovery is due almost entirely to her lying down several hours a day, during which time her stays were removed ...

Brisbane: Allow me to say a few words ... the ribs *enclose the chest*, in connection with the breastbone and spine, to which former ... seven principal ones are fastened by 'cartilages', which in childhood are elastic, but which ultimately become bone. Therefore, by the practice of putting children into stays at an early age, the lower ribs are pressed upon the heart and lungs, and their proper action is impeded ... I could say more, but a lady's paper is hardly the place for a medical discussion ...

An Inveterate Tight-lacer: From the absence of any correspondence on the all-important subject of tight-lacing in your August number, I very much fear that the subject has come to an end. If so, many other subscribers besides myself will be sorry for it. I cannot tell you what pleasure it gave me ... I quite agree with 'Staylace' ... to be tightly laced in a pair of stays is a most superb sensation ...

Miss E. Morris: Advises our readers to leave their stays alone. She says over-clothing is a great source of ill-health, and condemns *drawers* as being particularly injurious.

All from 'Conversazione', *The Englishwoman's Domestic Magazine*, 1867

Lottie: From your description, you are most likely suffering from nervousness and hysteria. Plenty of open-air exercise would be beneficial; and probably you require tonic medicine. We advise you to abstain from reading anything sensational, and to fix your thought on some useful and quiet occupation.

Lady Clare: Soak the feet in warm water, and pick the corn out with the point of a penknife.

Millicent: You have weakened your hair by not having it cut. The best plan will be to have it cut and singed, and to rub into the roots of the hair twice a week, a mixture of equal portions of rum and castor oil, shaken together.

All from *The Young Ladies' Journal*, 1875

Freckly Face: We are sorry to hear that you have any brothers so ill-bred and unkind and unmanly as to comment on your personal defects. Try 'never to mind'. There is no cure for freckles except to shut yourself up in a box. It is caused by a 'rusting' of the skin.

Clarrie: To wear a mackintosh to shelter you from the rain, taking it off after would not be unhealthy. If worn for too long it becomes a kind of vapour bath.

Daisy: Delicate people should be cautious in the use of cold water, as we have often before said.

A Country Clergyman's Daughter: You should adopt some gentle gymnastic exercises with the arms, which are said to be useful to the liver. Ten minutes, or less, before breakfast would be enough. See our answers to correspondents on the use of hot water to improve digestion.

All from *Girls' Own Paper*, 1884 and 1885

Intermittent Fever: The first indication is to get a *free* action of the bowels; give two 'Livingstone's Rousers' (Six grains each of Jalap and Rhubarb, with four grains of Calomel, and the same quantity of Quinine) at once.

The Travellers' Medical and Surgical Guide, 1888

Two Simple Ones: Are simple indeed if they take anything – such as vinegar and quack medicines – to make them thin. Why should you wear a false fringe of hair if you could cut your front hair a little shorter? The less you call in the use of shams of any kind, the better. But if you have lost hair and teeth, a wig and false set are very desirable.

Girls' Own Paper, 1891

Walter M: We are of the opinion that in this case the sleepwalking is caused by the disordered state of the stomach. A gentle laxative should be administered. Be careful not to awaken the child when you find him out of bed, but carry it carefully back.

Victorine: Never on any account administer laudanum to your little one without medical advice. No wonder you had great difficulty in arousing the child; it should be a great lesson to you.

Bow Legs: You cannot do better than use 'Tidman's Sea Salt'. If the leg becomes more bowed, have it examined.

Hypatia (Highgate): There is some danger of repetition of the attack, but the pills we subscribe will no doubt ward it off. We think the sewer gas has been the original cause of the trouble.

Limp: Many people suffer in the way you describe, but obtain relief by immediately jumping out of bed.

All from *The Physician, Enquire Within*, 1892 and 1893

Nil Desperandum: The out-flapping ears, so disfiguring, which we often see can be so easily prevented in childhood, that it is a wonder mothers do not give more thought to the matter. Children should be carefully watched, and never allowed to sleep without having the ears closely pressed to the head. Babies should always wear caps, then it will be impossible for their ears to assume such alarming and unbecoming shapes as frequently shock us.

A Matron, Enquire Within, 1893

Worried Violet: I am fifteen and am taken for ten. What can I do?

There is no need to despair, dear. There is plenty of time for you to grow yet. Practise swinging by your arms every day.

Aunt Marjorie, Home Sweet Home, 1893

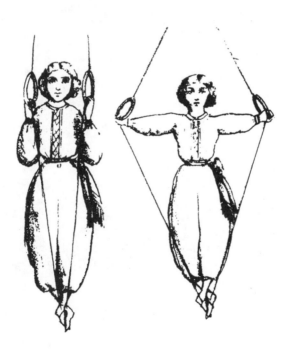

Ruby: *So* many of our girls complain of indigestion that we have taken the matter into serious consideration, and we recommend them to stiffen their dress bodices with whalebone and leave off wearing stays. Let the ribs expand well, and the process of digestion will not be interfered with. This is likewise our prescription for the red nose trouble. An extra woven vest would be an excellent substitute for stays because it would be elastic. You would all then approximate a little nearer to the classic forms of a Venus ...

Priscilla: Undoubtedly the best thing you can do is to leave your nose alone and not meddle with it. It will probably improve if left in peace.

Girls' Own Paper, 1894 and 1897

Ivy: Rub a little castor-oil nightly on the hard parts, and sleep in gloves.

The Young Woman, 1895

Hesperus: Do not feed your children on condensed milk alone. If you continue to do so you will have five rickety children to look after. Cow's milk, diluted with fresh barley water is the best artificial food for infants. Give the child with weak legs a little cream with her milk.

Miriam: We cannot too strongly insist upon the foolishness of taking patent medicines. How anyone can trifle with their health in this way, we cannot conceive. You are throwing into your blood a decoction of which you know nothing. You are feeding yourself upon drugs which, for all you know, may poison you. And what do you take these drugs for? Oh, for a headache or for biliousness! Of course we know that most patent medicines are inert; but only this morning a case is related in the newspapers of a woman who died from taking somebody's pills. Give up your silly habit of taking drugs at all. If you were not careless with your health you would probably not be suffering from your present troubles.

Anxious Alice: If you suffer from flatulence you must attend very carefully to your digestion and guard against constipation. A teaspoonful of liquorice powder will suffice … The pain of wind may often be relieved by taking half a teaspoonful of spirit of ginger. Six miles a day is sufficient exercise.

Carnation enquires: 'Are tomatoes healthy?'
That as an article of food, they conduce to our
health is absolutely proved. Few vegetables are
more wholesome. Ladies do not rise, if seated,
when gentlemen address them.

Endymion: There is not the slightest objection to
your marrying because you have had pneumonia.

Mystic: Beer poured over a red-hot horseshoe
will not cure dyspepsia. On the contrary, it will
make it worse.

Girls' Own Paper, 1899

Schoolboy vice: Have you not a family doctor
you can trust? Glad indeed that you have seen the
terrible error. Yes, there is an operation for the
evil after-effects; but I don't think it is necessary in
your case. The cold bath every morning and take
plenty of good, non-stimulating food.

More school vice: I credit you, however, with
honest bulldog pluck and staying power ... that
having made a fixed and determined resolve to get
rid of any bad habits, smoking or anything worse

and more fatal, though you may stumble, and fall many times, you will not quit hold. Having laid hold of the plough, you will not look behind you …

Dr Gordon Stables, Boys' Own Paper, 1899 and
1902

Immediate treatment to attempt to defer Tropical Fever: Sometimes violent exertion, producing perspiration and exhaustion, if practised in time, may avert an attack. We hear of a doctor visiting a man when the shivering fit was about to come on, who locked the door, mixed two glasses of stiff hot grog, put on the gloves, and engaged his patient in a boxing match, which, for that time at least, averted the fever.

*W.H. Lord and T. Baines, Shifts and
Expedients of Camp Life,* 1876

Alice: The lady who offered a cure for nasal catarrh has requested me not to give her address again, as it has involved her in more correspondence than she has time for.

The Young Woman, 1900

Little Dutch Girl: If you wish to grow stouter drink plenty of milk. Get some cod-liver oil and rub your chest with it every night before bed. To help to increase your figure, buy a 'Sandow's Developer'. Screw the hook into the woodwork in your bedroom, and after a bath, go through a few of the exercises described.

Girls' Own Paper, 1907

Would-Be Water Lily and Worried Molly: If you do that mad thing again of drinking 'a small tumblerful of vinegar' to make yourselves thin you will only have yourselves to thank if you are seriously ill.

Mary Marryat, Woman's Weekly, 1920

Mrs. F.A. (Liverpool): I am much troubled on account of my bad eyesight. I think it is from steam from the cooking I do. Do you think this is so? If so what can I do?

You don't mention your age, or if the amount of cooking you do is very great. I think it is very unlikely that steam has anything to do with your eyesight. Most likely you simply need glasses.

Too Fat P.T.: Please tell me how to reduce my fat. Will massage and cold sponges do any good? I am twenty and lead an active life. How can I get my hip bones back to a normal position? They stick out.

Girls of twenty should not go in for reducing diets – but you could avoid potatoes, cakes and sweets. You might try massage, but, I fear, it will be of little use. As for the removal of bones that 'stick out' – this is beyond my province. I would strongly counsel you to leave well alone and not attempt experiments with your bones.

Florence Stackpoole, 'Ask Me', from Mother and Home, 1915

Ronnie from Glasgow writes: Thank you for your help. Without doubt it is the most comfortable appliance of its kind. Kindly send another. My wife was so pleased with the results of mine that she would like to try one, too.

Modern, 1926

Desperate Maud: I am very sorry for you and urge you to make a big effort and pull yourself together and to stop this slackness and lassitude. At forty-five no woman ought to go under as you say. There is no reason why you should be ill or feel ill. Certainly pay no attention to a friend who advises you to take stout, as you are not accustomed to intoxicants; you should avoid all food and drink that fatten. Will you write to me privately? I can then say more than I can do here.

Mabel (Ilford): Suspenders are very preferable to garters, but if you prefer the latter, wear them below the knee. I may say, however, they tend to impede the circulation.

The Shadow Woman's Post Bag, Woman's
Friend, 1925

Worried Mother: I have a daughter of seventeen and she has started smoking. I think smoking is bad for girls, but she says that if it is not bad for boys, it is not bad for girls. Will you give me your opinion?

I will give you the opinion of experienced doctors who say that smoking is not good for boys or girls. It is bad for the eyes, the heart, and the digestion. It is also bad for the complexion.

Ignorant Betty: I am getting married shortly and have asked my mother to tell me the intimate facts of life. She says I am thoroughly nasty and morbid and shall find out soon enough. Can you help me?

Send a stamped, addressed envelope and I will tell you all you need to know.

Mrs Marryat Advises, Woman's Weekly, 1926

Miscellaneous

'Of mixed composition or character.'
The Shorter Oxford English Dictionary

N ow we come to the delightful section that is the rag-bag of human enquiry. Here can be found a range of the most original, puzzling and curious questions, all answered with helpful conviction. An agony aunt who could turn a hand to anything was obviously a great asset to the printed page. Be it as solicitor, teacher, beautician, gardener, housekeeper, tourist guide or games player ~ the list is endless ~ in the early years of their existence dedicated, problem-solving aunties and uncles always had an answer (or comment) up their sleeve ... to anyone, for everything.

TO CORRESPONDENTS

Questions and Answers Concerning
*A Variety of Philosophical
and Practical Subjects Including Beauty,
Singing, Handwriting, Fashion, Neelework,
Housewifery, Law and Order, Child-Rearing
and Bicycling*

Sir: A certain person on Sunday last, in the sermon time was drinking in an ale house where he dined, for which he was forced to pay 3 shillings and 6 pence. Yet the Justice of Peace, who caused the man to pay the said money, was the same day tippling himself in sermon time.

Now I would fain know what treatment this said Justice ought to meet with, and to whom may a man safely go to inform against him; for without any doubt no Justice will fine or condemn a Justice, but rather send the informer to prison; therefore what ought to be done in this case, that the Reformation may take its free course?

Sir: Have no doubt that this Justice can be judged by his fellow Justices if the information appears to be the truth.

The Athenian Oracle, c. 1697

I have received a letter, desiring me to be very satirical upon the little muff that is now in fashion; another informs me of a pair of silver garters buckled below the knee, that have been lately seen at the Rainbow coffee-house in Fleet-street; a third sends me a heavy complaint against fringed gloves. To be brief, there is scarce an ornament of either sex which one or other of my correspondents has not inveighed against with some bitterness, and recommended to my observation. I must therefore, once for all, inform my readers, that it is not my intention to sink the dignity of this my paper with reflections upon red-heels or top-knots, but rather enter into the passions of mankind, and to correct those depraved sentiments that gave birth to all those little extravagancies which appear in their outward dress and behaviour. Foppish and fantastic ornaments are only indications of vice, not criminal in themselves. Extinguish vanity in the mind, and you naturally retrench the little superfluities of garniture and equipage. The blossoms will fall by themselves when the root that nourishes them is destroyed.

The Spectator, 1711

There is another set of correspondents to whom I must address myself... I mean such as fill their letters with private scandal, and black accounts of particular persons and families. The world is so full of ill-nature, that I have lampoons sent me by people who cannot spell, and satires composed by people who scarce know how to write. By the last post in particular I received a packet of scandal which is not legible; and have a whole bundle of letters, in women's hands that are full of blots ... insomuch, that when I see the name Celia, Phillis, Pastora, or the like, at the bottom of a scrawl, I conclude ... that it brings me some account of a fallen virgin, a faithless wife, or an amorous widow. I must therefore inform ... it is not my design to bring little infamous stories out of their present lurking-holes into broad daylight.

The Spectator, 1711

Sir: My wife has gone mad! What is worse, politically mad! Ever since the commencement of the Westminster election my wife has been intoxicated with politics, my servants with strong beer, and my house has resounded with nothing but 'Fox for ever!' It would have been some consolation had she confined her folly to her own house, but alas! She has been canvassing with a vengeance! And with petting one fellow, kissing another and coaxing with thousands has driven me almost horn-mad! ... she should remember that female reputation is of slender contexture and that 'To her belongs the care to shun the blast of slanderous tongues'.

This, however, is impossible so long as she interferes in matters which by no means concern her or her sex ...

The gentleman ... is indeed too fond and too indulgent in permitting his wife to disgrace herself by conduct so reprehensible. If reasoning fails, he should hurry her into the country and, by taking her from the scene of the action, endeavour to reclaim her. It has, of late years, been too much the vogue amongst the fashionable fair to imitate in everything the other sex, particularly in modes of dress and matters of amusement.

The New Spectator, 1784

While I recommend that the rouge, we sparingly permit, should be laid on with delicacy, my readers must not suppose that I intend such advice as a means of making the art a deception. It seems to me so slight and so innocent an apparel of the face (a kind of decent veil thrown over the cheek, rendered too eloquent of grief by the pallidness of secret sorrow) that I cannot see any shame in the most ingenuous female acknowledging that she occasionally rouges. It is often, like a cheerful smile on the face of an invalid, put on to give comfort to an anxious friend.

A Lady of Distinction, The Mirror of Graces,

1811

I am nineteen, have had a boarding-school education; speak French ... play the piano ... dance, draw and do ornamental needlework. My papa is a haberdasher, and wants me to stand in his shop; and I wish to ask whether I ought? And what is the use of an education like mine if instead of making an advantage of it, I am to forget it all, by mixing with shop men and measure tape like a dowdy? My mama says it is wrong, and as my papa can give me very little fortune, he ought to exhibit me as much as possible with all my accomplishments; the only chance I have of moving in my proper sphere is by getting a rich man. Please give me your advice ...

If your education has been sound you will not lose it by mixing with shop women, and measuring tape; by assisting your father, you are endeavouring to make some return for his indulgence. I have omitted shop men because I think a young lady of such a mind as yours appears to be, might be in some danger amongst them, and I am sorry to find you can write shop men ... there are few employments for females and so many out of bread I think it will be a great shame that men are engaged at all to do that which appears to be the peculiar province of our sex — but for this our sex are to blame, for which I shall give my reasons in a future paper.

The Lady's Magazine, 1817

It is part of the plan of this publication to give details of Fashionable occurrences at the Provincial Places of Resort so that Readers, who Enquire, may decide upon their suitability as a Seasonal Retreat.

We tell of Brighton: The arrivals in this delightful town have very much increased and many of the best lodging-houses have received fashionable tenants for lengthened periods. *'Lodgings to Let'* placards have disappeared and good houses, in the best approved and expensive situations, are, at this time, in pleasing requisition. A new Swimming-Bath has been opened here. The basin is circular, and with a diameter of 53 feet, by a circumference of nearly 162; the descent, by steps, is safe and easy. In the centre, a fountain rises, which is constantly supplying the basin with water from the sea. The action of the fountain is such, that a ripple animates the surface of the Bath, the contents of which, often renewed, have a freshness imparted equal to that of the ocean itself. Ten dressing-rooms, suitably furnished, open to the steps of the bath, entirely private and distinct from each other.

The World of Fashion, 1824

Dolly Varden: 'Old Maid' is for the most part a term of insult, and unwarrantable. The appropriate term is 'a maiden lady', and the age may, or may not, be added.

Emily: 1. We are not aware that anything has yet been discovered for *preventing* the hair turning grey; but it is possible to convert grey hair to black or brown, by means of various dyes, several of which, of a perfectly *harmless* kind, we have occasionally submitted to our readers. 2. We can suggest no better method of cleaning chinchilla fur than that we recommended last week in our reply to 'Bianca'.

Angelina: 1. Certainly the earrings and brooch mentioned, may, with perfect good taste, be worn with a gold chain. 2. The price of a steel chatelaine is from two to five guineas. They may be obtained, in great variety, at Durham's, 453, New Oxford-street, near Bedford Chapel.

Bella Donna: In conducting a lady down stairs to dinner, the rule is for the gentleman to give the lady the wall, and not the banister.

Christine: A curtsy, or polite inclination of the head, is the only ceremony to be observed on the occasion in question. If the lady should be disposed to show a token of civility, it is for her to offer her hand. The gentleman might naturally suppose it would be presumption on his part to do so.

Judy: Steep it in *boiling* water.

Florinda Blanche: We believe it will be found that the constant use of tweezers will, ultimately, prove the most effectual way for removing superfluous hairs.

Teresa: Curling-irons for the waved bandeaux may be had at Mr. Rossi's, 254, Regent-street.

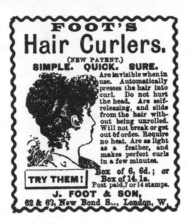

Rose-Coloured Tarletan: The dress should be made with a great number of tucks graduated in width, from the lower one upwards, or with flounces scalloped at the edges and set on nearly plain. The flounces may be edged with braid or with very narrow satin puffing. Over white satin, a double skirt of tarletan has not a pretty effect.

Janet Geraldine: Powdered French chalk rubbed well on the spots of grease and allowed to remain a few days and then brushed, is the best thing to be used.

Erminia: We know of no book on the subject. Our advice is, leave Fate alone.

Jane Eyre: Watered silk will be found most useful for the lining. The cord and tassels must be of a colour to harmonize with the damask of the cushion.

Lady Maria: 1. Very tall. 2. Rather dark. 3. No, but by no means handsome. 4. No, no, no.

All from *The Lady's Newspaper,* 1848 and 1849

Letitia: It is not unusual. Many orators have a similar habit. Madame de Stael could never enter into an intellectual combat without something to occupy her hands. It was her custom always to have a twig of poplar with two or three leaves on it, which she invariably twirled about, as a sort of accompaniment to her words. She used to declare that she should be dumb without it, and even when she went to parties some substitute was always provided.

Verbena: Try the following directions for extracting grease spots from velvet: Warm the spot before the fire, then hold it over the finger, and carefully apply spirits of wine with a silk handkerchief.

A Nervous Lady: In many of the principal

thoroughfares of both the West-end and the City, to cross the streets in safety, requires both presence of mind and quickness of action. We think the subject demands attention. It would be perfectly easy for the police to regulate the conveyances so that at stated intervals a pause of a minute or two should take place to enable pedestrians to cross in numbers together, at those points where the stream of vehicles is continuous and the danger greatest.

All from *The Lady's Newspaper*, 1859

Nanny: We do not tell characters by handwriting; your writing is not good, whatever your character may be.

A Constant Subscriber (Haverstock-hill) wishes to reply to Stella's questions in 'Conversazione', that by boiling her discoloured pearls in soapsuds for a few minutes she can restore their colour. To Stella's second question, A Constant Subscriber would recommend Duncan and Flockhart's prepared guttapercha as a permanent stopping for decayed teeth.

Evelyn: Your behaviour in a ballroom should be what we hope it is everywhere, quiet and ladylike. Nothing is more injurious to a girl than being 'talked about'.

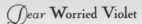

The following correspondents would be glad to receive answers from other correspondents in our columns:

Bertha would like to know a method for curing stammering.

Jessica wants to know the best way of cultivating the voice for singing in public.

E.F.M. would like the opinion of friends on the prettiest and most becoming dress for a bride – brunette, *petite*.

An English Mama: Many naughty children are only to be startled into better conduct by sudden corporal punishment. In your case, we advise you at the first act of disobedience to administer a sharp box on the ear or *hard* slap; if this fails, have recourse to the remedy you propose, but be sure it is severe, and in the old-fashioned style; a good birch of twigs hurts more and injures less than the hand or rod. If a 'good sound whipping' fails you are in a worse plight than before, and school is the only chance of breaking a troublesome girl. Absence from home and school trials and hardships have wrought wonders. The whipping ought to be managed by yourself alone, without help or witnesses.

A.B. sends us some verses. As *we* have had the agony of reading them, we revenge ourselves on our readers by printing a verse from two of the poems with which she has favoured us ...

My Own Native Valley

I've seen roaring cascades
Flow down some huge hill,
All foaming and dashing,
And never is still.

I Love to Roam

Any day he may come, back again to his home,
So I'm watching, watching the sea,
And the time seems long, as I wander along,
For he's very dear to me.

All from 'Conversazione', The Englishwoman's
Domestic Magazine, 1867

Aquarium: We quite understand from your description the disease that has attacked your goldfish; but we are unable to tell you the cause. Purchase some more.

Mona: It is a rule to wear deep mourning for parents for a year, and slight mourning for the second year.

Piccolo Regina: The way to make a postage-stamp snake – the stamps must be strung on purse-silk. They are cut very small at the tail, gradually getting larger towards the head. The snake should be rather more than a yard in length. The head is made of gray silk, lined with scarlet, a tongue projecting.

Amy Robsart: 1. Many young widows would cease to wear mourning entirely after two years. 2. Mourning of any kind is out of place at a wedding; do not attend or wear something more suitable.

Dagmar: Girls of fourteen very often attempt to write verses. When they get a little older, they resolve to spend their time more profitably. We are inclined to think that will be your case.

All from *The Young Ladies' Journal*, 1874

Ball-Room Decoration, Gloucester: I would suggest a few yards of pink calico and white muslin for 'Puppy''s ball-room, fastened here and there with great bunches of common ferns. Pink and white paper roses might also be mixed with foliage to make festoons or wreaths. Chinese lanterns also look well; the raised platform upon which the musicians sit might be draped with something red, ornamented with pots of greenhouse flowers. All green looks well at night. I have seen gooseberry bushes, hung with lamps, look quite artistic in the dark.

A correspondent, Petronella, says to E.M.S.: a good sized crust of bread boiled with greens, will prevent any disagreeable smell from them. No lid must be put on the saucepan.

A Lady who Frets: As a present for a gentleman, a lathe affords endless variety of amusement. The Britannia Company offer the most perfect machine. Price from 17 shillings on a strong stand to work by foot. Apply the Amateur Tool Department, Colchester.

Emily asks about Tennis Dress: What material would be most suitable? It must be inexpensive, washable and capable of being worked with crewels. Also what flower is likely to be fashionable to work on it?

I should recommend fine flannel, *voile religieuse*, cashmere or Umritza as suitable materials. Fruit is more fashionable than flowers for ornamentation; in our opinion, pomegranates are most favoured.

Jesset: Directions wanted for keeping the ivory keys of a piano white. Is it best to keep the piano closed or open?

Closed, if you wish to keep the dust out.

Trousseau for Calcutta: Fuller particulars have appeared in *The Queen*, under the heads, Outfit for India and Boots for India. 'Gertrude' would be far more satisfied if she has her clothes placed in tin-lined cases, soldered down. The sea and heat are sad enemies.

All from *'Answers', 'The Queen', The Lady's Newspaper*, 1882

Little Fairy: To cure creaking boots, take them to a shoemaker and get him to spring them on each side and insert, between the soles, a teaspoonful of French chalk. This should cure the mischief.

Flageolet: There is no reason why you should not play the flute. To adopt the trombone, bassoon or big drum might look somewhat out of character for a delicate, small girl. Besides, your neighbours might see additional objections.

Disheartened: If you again send us a letter written in such a horrible hand, we shall certainly not attempt to decipher it. As a great favour we have made the attempt this time. *Of course,* those *first* intermarried until the privilege of selection became extended. There was then no inherited disease to render such unions destructive. When God saw fit to prohibit their continuance, it then became a crime to make them. Wear gloves.

Nobody's Own: We sympathize with you on the destruction of your umbrella. Your late mistress acted very improperly, even dishonestly, in lending it to workmen until broken to pieces; but

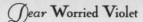

it will teach you not to leave things behind. We hope you will be happy in your new place.

All from *Girls' Own Paper,* 1884–1885

This publication was a fearlessly progressive, evangelical and educational magazine for girls of all classes.

Old Fashion: Starch was first brought into England by Mrs Dinghein, a Fleming, May 1st, 1653. Mrs Anne Turner, a milliner, introduced from France the French custom of using yellow starch in getting up bands and ruffs, and it was applied to the huge ruffs then worn. She was afterwards concerned in the murder of Sir Thomas Overbury, and was hung. She appeared, by Lord Coke's order, on the scaffold with a large ruff, and this put an end to this ugly fashion, as he had no doubt intended to do.

Miss H. Poland: Thank you for your letter. We are happy to inform our readers that you are the secretary of that much-to-be-approved-of Society for the Protection of Birds. It is required of members that they shall not wear the feathers of any bird not killed for food, the ostrich excepted. It is satisfactory to observe that a large proportion of birds worn in hats are only artificial, made up with stray feathers on a sham foundation ~ a new industry for needy workers. The preservation of our birds, whether singers or not, should be a matter of strict legislation ~ and the destruction of seagulls very particularly, as they are not only harmless, but actively useful.

Tea-Rose and Heliotrope: Green and all shades of brown are much worn at present.

Connie: You cannot write properly, so you could not teach children; and we have no means of judging for what else you have any capabilities.

Fanny, Margaret and Arthur: Special probationers are received at the Charing Cross Hospital for not less than one year at one guinea a week. At St Bartholomew's Hospital, E.C., they are received for periods of three months at £13 13 shillings. Write in all cases to the Matron.

Minerva: Your question is rather absurd. What do you say when you receive a present? Say that you feel much obliged for it, or simply the words 'Thank you' ~ and look smiling and as gracious as you can, not with the glum expression of a bulldog, or even a cow. Wedding cake deserves kindly thanks as well as anything else. It is the habit of young people to sleep on a scrap of it, to give them such dreams as they desire. Of course, this is only child's play, no prophecy of future matrimonial prospects could be obtained through the influence of a piece of cake. Your writing is more 'childish' than 'boyish'.

Etiquette: You should not have asked him in to take any meal without having obtained your mother's consent. She would then have remained at home, or declined to allow your invitation. You had no right to 'do the honours'. Your sister should have remained in the room until he left.

Tag: Sponging with a little cold tea will restore black ribbon and black lace.

Belfast Reader: We sympathize with you as regards the annoyance which you meet from the impertinence of idle young men who stare at and speak to you on your leaving the School of Art evening classes at half-past nine, and while waiting for an omnibus to take you home. Could you not get some fellow students to come out with you and wait a few minutes beside you? It might be well to inform the authorities of the school of the annoyance awaiting your leaving, and they would communicate with the police to protect the students waiting outside for conveyance. It is indeed a disgrace to those who take so low and unmanly an advantage of a respectable woman.

All from *Girls' Own Paper,* 1891

Corset: There is a knitted woollen corset made that would be the very make you require. It is well adapted to young girls' wear. Ask for it at any underlinen shop or ladies' outfitters.

LADIES' UNDERLINEN.

Nuisance Rose: I quite understand the unfortunate position in which you are placed with regard to your downstairs neighbour, but the only means open to you is through your landlord. Of course your children have a right to play the piano in your own rooms, and I think you are very considerate in making them remove their boots when they come indoors.

A little roll of white paper, inserted through the upper-crust of the pie, will prevent the juice from being forced out into the oven

Half a teaspoonful of sugar will nearly always revive a dying fire, and unlike the few drops of paraffin, which servants are so fond of using, is perfectly safe.

Remedy for Perspiration: If those who perspire freely would use a little ammonia in the water they bathe in each day, it would keep their flesh clean and sweet, doing away with disagreeable odour.

Black beetles: Emma writes in answer ~ I am very pleased to tell 'Annie' how I got rid of black beetles with which my house was infested. I mixed a cupful of plaster of Paris with two cupfuls of oatmeal and spread it about the floor. Numbers lay dead every morning.

'An Aunt': We are much pleased you appreciate our paper so highly; we are always glad to hear from our readers. We do not advocate whipping, but the case you mention seems an exceptionable one. You say pain is the only thing the child fears, therefore we recommend you procure a birch rod, and administer a whipping when he next offends. Avoid locking him up alone in a room; it seldom results in any good, and often leads to mischief.

'Adopted Daughter': The parents of the child certainly can claim her return at any time they wish while she is under age.

All from *'Enquire Within', Ladies' Home Journal*, 1893

'I am to be married in February,' Kathlyn Bryan tells me, 'and in my travelling-dress. Do you think a Royal blue would look pretty, as blue suits me so well? I am going to have a bicycle. Mother doesn't quite take to ladies cycling yet; so when my fiancé wanted to buy me one I had to explain, and he said, as he would be taking me from her so soon, we must please her for the time I was still with her. Now she says I must do as he likes, so I am to have my bicycle, and I'm just the happiest girl alive!'

I think Royal blue would look very nice, and could have a fur-trimmed cape to go with it. Lack of space prevents giving you a full list for your trousseau. How nice about the bicycle. You have my hearty congratulations.

'White Violet': You have failed to observe our rule respecting the stamped envelope. We are, in consequence, unable to forward the information you so desperately require.

'Two Schoolgirls' are 'perfectly sick' of tennis and croquet, and ask me to suggest a different game for next spring.

Try fives. It is a capital game for girls, and

brings the muscles into action in a manner which I am sure your family doctor would thoroughly approve.

'Can you', enquires 'Blue Roses' 'give me any hints about getting up a bicycle gymkhana, or musical ride? We want something of the sort this winter for local charities, and there is a big drill-hall where we can hold it. But though we are all very keen on cycling here, none of us know how to get up anything of the kind.'

I can tell you the very help you need! There is a book just published called 'Bicycle Gymkhana and Musical Rides'. It is written by Major Walter Wingfield, of the Royal Bodyguard, the inventor of lawn-tennis, and will tell you all you want to know.

'Now that the hunting season is in full swing,' says 'Microbe', 'I have rather a difficulty to solve. We have had to put down one of our hunters, and can no longer mount a groom to go with me. I have no father or brother, and my mother has scruples about letting me go out alone with an elderly, married neighbour who has known me all my life.'

There is no reason in the world why he should not look after you. It is perfectly correct as he is an elderly, married man, and family friend. Your mother need not worry. I sympathize with you in your reluctance to give up hunting. It is delightful, isn't it? I don't wonder you are so fond of it.

'It would be a great help to me,' says 'T.P.', 'if you would be good enough to tell me, in your particular page, if it is possible to kill worms that have got into some oak furniture I bought. The chairs are modern ones, but have come from an old house. What had I better do to prevent further damage? Also please tell me if it is a sign a bride is ready to receive callers when she appears in church on Sunday?'

Yes ~ to the last question. Now about the first one. What you call worms is really dry-rot ... a terrible infectious disorder which, if not checked, will probably cause the furniture to crumble to dust. You should soak the chairs thoroughly in paraffin ~ it is the only thing to destroy the insects.

'Can you tell me what kind of outfit I will need for Malta?' asks 'Flighty'. 'I have been invited to spend the end of the winter with friends in the garrison out there. They go out a great deal. Do people dress much? And do I need furs and warm things?'

You will find the winter climate like May or September at home; but it grows rapidly hot in the spring. Winter frocks are generally worn, without a jacket, except on exceptional days. Blue serge or tweed coats and skirts for day wear, with a smarter frock for races and receptions. Plenty of evening gowns for the opera and balls, and a fancy dress for the carnival ball at the Palace. No; people dress very simply.

All from 'Side Talks with Girls' by Lady Betty,
Home Chat, 1897

Myrtle: The machine you have is a good one, but I believe it would not be advisable to start in on a third season with added strains. Better to sell it, and get a good free wheel with ratchet clutch and rim-brakes. With regard to the back-pedalling brake, considerable difference of opinion exists, but ladies, as a rule, prefer it as it is easier to hold on to down long hills.

The Queen, 1900

Desolate: I am afraid it is impossible to advise you without knowing something of the circumstances. Do you mean to imply that your friend has been spirited away against his will? In any case, I do not see how you could possibly increase your chances of tracing him by taking such a dangerous situation as you suggest. It would be unwise to proceed.

Cliftonian: There is a home for elderly ladies not far from you. Write for a prospectus. Lynwood, Brentwood, Essex. Terms from £26 yearly.

Both from *The Lady*, 1901

The Merry Widow: This writing shows good temper and a highly sympathetic temperament. He has much interest in women, and he has a great power of attachment. The signature to this study shows a passionate nature and the capitals an artistic perception of beauty.

Lady's Pictorial, 1906

Absolutely Alone: Would you give up your house and go and live with another lady? It seems so wretched for you to go on living in a house by yourself where you cannot afford to keep a servant. We know of a lady living near Staines who is looking out for another lady to share her house. She would let three rooms – one of these a large, sunny front room, opening on to a balcony, fully furnished, for 11 shillings a week. You would have to feed yourself and pay your share for coal and gas. It seems to us an impossible struggle for you to go on in your own house on the small income you possess. You could let your house and sell some of the furniture. If you think this plan will suit you, write to us again, giving your name and address (*not for publication*), and we will try to arrange an interview with the lady.

'Answers', Girls' Own Paper, 1907

Mrs Brown of Beeston tells me: I never throw old mackintoshes away. Rather I cut them up into aprons, which I find most useful when scrubbing floors, washing up the dishes or on wash days.

Mrs Varley of Lancaster says: Red flannel has a strong attraction for moths, so, after putting winter garments away, leave a square of flannel on the floor of the cupboard and the moths will eat this in preference to anything else.

From *'Found Out', Woman's Own*, 1913

Who is Mary? Mary is EVERYWOMAN'S Human encyclopaedia: it is her mission in life to answer everywoman's every question. If domestic, business or social problems trouble you, don't worry. Instead, ask Mary – she knows. Mary will give a definite answer to every letter sent to her. **A prize of 10s 6d each week will be awarded for the most interesting letter.**

This week it is awarded to Miss Matley, 15 Kenworthy Street, Stalybridge. She writes:

Dear Mary, – Rather impertinence on my part, calling you that, but you are to me – just Mary. I want to tell you how pleased I am that you are now included in Everywoman's, which is such a chummy paper. I look forward to Mondays as the best day of the week, for it brings Everywoman's. I enjoy it all, from the Gossip to the Cookery, but your page is best of all.

Just at the moment I have nothing to ask you, but if ever I am in trouble I shall write at once. In the meantime, I just want to know you, and you to know me.

Everywoman, 1928

Unhappy Olive: Buy a chiffon or gauze veil, and wear it whenever the wind is cold. On no account try massaging your nose. Wear warm stockings, stout, comfortable shoes and woollen underwear.

Elizabeth (Manchester): If some of your things have got badly faded and yet you don't want to make them white, a few drops of red ink added to the rinsing water will give you a delicate pink, or a warm coral, red and blue ink, a dainty lilac, and strong coffee, a lovely daffodil yellow.

The prize of 2s 6d for the best hint is awarded to Mrs Lloyd, 43, Silverleigh Road, Thornton Heath:

This is an easy way of emptying a feather bed into a new ticking. Leave an opening at one end, about half-yard. Open the old tick the same length, tack the two together and shake feathers in. This can be done in a room with no mess.

Woman's Weekly, 1921–25

Perplexed: On two occasions oysters have been served me as the first course at a dinner. Can you tell me what is the correct way these should be eaten?

You should take the fork in your right hand and take the oyster up with it. The oysters served at dinner are always the small 'native' oysters and can be popped into the mouth whole. Thin brown bread and butter is the usual accompaniment.

All from *Woman's Weekly,* 1921 and 1925

Chic Bertha: How can I keep my new shingled hair neat and sleek during the night?

Get one of the new shingle caps. These are very pretty, light and cool to wear. They have ear pieces to flatten your side curls and tie under the chin so that it doesn't slide about in bed.

Modern, 1926

Distressed: Can you recommend a quick-working reducing cream? My chest is much too large for my liking. I cannot run to a reducing roller, unfortunately.

Chests *must not* be rolled. Nor do we advise dosing with cream. This particular bit of the anatomy is very easily injured. Take my advice and try the effect of a cross-over brassiere.

Woman's Weekly, 1927